Original title:
This Time You Return To Yourself

Copyright © 2024 Book Fairy Publishing
All rights reserved.

Editor: Theodor Taimla
Author: Samira Siil
ISBN HARDBACK: 978-9916-759-10-3
ISBN PAPERBACK: 978-9916-759-11-0

Rediscovered Truths

In shadows cast by evening hues,
A whisper soft, a time to muse,
The hidden paths we never choose,
Lead back again to olden truths.

Beneath the stars, the night unveils,
The stories wrapped in twilight veils,
Forgotten dreams and ancient tales,
In silent whispers, heart prevails.

The echoes of the past, they call,
Through time and space, a gentle sprawl,
With wisdom found in one and all,
To rise, to stand, and never fall.

The winds of change, they sweep anew,
To cleanse the old and forge the true,
Yet what remains in morning dew,
Are seeds of light in shades of blue.

In every heart, a beacon shines,
A compass set by stars that bind,
With every step, the soul aligns,
Rediscovered truths, in paths we find.

Sanctum of Serendipity

In the garden of moonlit dreams,
Whispers dance like gleaming streams,
Through the tapestry of chance,
Weaves the thread of circumstance.

Silent shadows softly play,
Guiding feet in night and day,
Fortune's hand and fate's decree,
Shaping what is meant to be.

Mystic winds and starlit skies,
Lead us where the heart complies,
In this realm where wonders lie,
Every breath a lullaby.

Dawn of Awareness

As the night surrenders light,
Truth emerges from the night,
Breaking bonds of world's disguise,
In the morn of new surmise.

Echoes fade as silence grows,
Inner wisdom freely flows,
Eyes once shut now wide perceive,
Endless realms where thoughts conceive.

Morning's gold on dewdrops shine,
Hints of secrets held divine,
Awake the soul in dawn's embrace,
Journey forth with newfound grace.

Convergence of Being

Paths converge beneath the sky,
Souls aligned in silent cry,
Harmonize as one heart's beat,
In the place where spirits meet.

Threads of life entwine and weave,
Shared destiny we all believe,
Boundaries fade in this serene,
Unified, we are supreme.

Echoes of the past recede,
In this moment, hearts are freed,
One existence, all converge,
Life's pure essence, we emerge.

Truth's Quiet Echo

In the hall of whispered words,
Silent truths begin to surge,
Through the quiet, soft and clear,
Echoes linger, drawing near.

Secrets hidden in the veil,
Beneath the noise that often fails,
Quiet shadows softly speak,
Granting strength to those who seek.

Gently falls the night's embrace,
Unveils the truth with gentle grace,
Hearing what the heart can't show,
In the echo, wisdom flows.

Harmony's Revival

A songbird's call in morning light,
Brushes dew from grass so bright,
Sunrise paints the sky alight,
Whisperings of day's delight.

Streams through valleys gently wind,
Chasing dreams we long to find,
Nature's symphony, unlined,
A dance of soul and mind.

Leaves in whispered conversation,
Winds of subtle implication,
Unity in grand ovation,
Harmony's sweet proclamation.

Whispered Realizations

Moonlight weaves its silver beams,
Through the tapestry of dreams,
In the hush, life softly gleams,
Unraveling its silent schemes.

Stars align in quiet grace,
Patterns in the cosmic space,
Truth unfolds at measured pace,
In whispers we embrace.

Questions float on twilight air,
In this stillness, secrets share,
Realizations pure and rare,
In whispers laid bare.

Glimmer of Self-Knowledge

Mirror's depth, a soul's reflection,
Paths to inner introspection,
Finding truth in dark affection,
Glimmers of self-perfection.

Whispers in the shadowed night,
Guiding toward a modest light,
Inner compass, shining bright,
Onward to the self's insight.

Journey through the mind's terrain,
Gains and losses, joy and pain,
In this search, we truly gain,
Knowledge pure and unfeigned.

Rekindling the Flame

Once in ashes, sparks concealed,
Hope in embers much revealed,
Time the wounds began to heal,
   Flame of life again to feel.

Kindlings of joy intertwine,
Moments fleeting, yet divine,
Hearts and souls in tender line,
   Passions fervent fire define.

Rise anew from long despair,
Love and light born in the air,
Flame rekindled, spirit rare,
Bound in warmth beyond compare.

Roots of Renewal

In the silence of the forest deep,
Whispers of the old trees speak.
Their roots in earth, ancient and wise,
Nourish the dreams that in them lie.

Rise through the soil, new shoots green,
Life reborn in nature's serene.
Stretch and grow toward the sky,
Embrace the cycles, do not defy.

Seasons shift, the leaves must fall,
Yet spring returns to paint them all.
Beneath the frost, hope's seeds laid,
In patience waiting, unafraid.

An Odyssey Inward

Journey within the soul's deep core,
Find the truths we've long ignored.
Winding paths through thoughts we've sown,
Each step reveals a world unknown.

Dive beyond the surface bright,
Into shadows, to seek the light.
In silence, hear the heart's own quest,
The inward odyssey knows best.

Layers peel, unveiling scars,
Wounds that heal beneath the stars.
In the quiet, stillness reigns,
Peace is born from inner gains.

Guardian of Silence

In the quiet realms of night,
A guardian stands beyond the light.
Listening to stars that sing,
Guarding dreams on whispering wings.

Shadows fall, a tranquil hush,
Silence speaks in twilight's blush.
Veil of stillness, soft embrace,
A sanctuary, timeless space.

Echoes rest in calm's own keep,
Where secrets in the silence sleep.
In the heart, this guardian dwells,
Keeping tales that silence tells.

Cherished Moments Inside

In the warmth of a quiet room,
Dreams and memories start to bloom.
Moments shared, both bright and sweet,
In these walls, our hearts repeat.

Laughter echoes through the space,
Love's own rhythm, time can't erase.
Songs of joy and whispered sighs,
Cherished moments never die.

Within these bounds, our lives entwine,
Simple treasures, pure and fine.
Hold them close, as shadows fade,
In our hearts, they will be laid.

The Path Back Inward

Starlit skies and quiet nights,
Guide this journey of the heart.
In the stillness, find the light,
Where inner worlds can start.

Gentle whispers of the breeze,
Carry secrets from within.
Feel the softness, be at ease,
Let the healing now begin.

Bit by bit, the veil unveils,
Hidden truths and worlds anew.
Broken paths and distant trails,
Lead you back to being true.

Serenity in Self-Discovery

In the hush of morning's grace,
Find the whispers of your soul.
Through the quiet, find your place,
Hearts in pieces become whole.

Every step, a new reveal,
Hidden facets open wide.
Learn to trust in what you feel,
Let your instincts be your guide.

As the dawn breaks soft and clear,
Embrace the essence of your 'you'.
Shed the layers without fear,
Discover peace in what is true.

Whispering Echoes of Truth

Upon the winds, the truth does ride,
In whispers soft, its secrets told.
Through the shadows, find your guide,
In the echoes, stories old.

Listen close to what is near,
In the silence, wisdom flows.
Banish every doubt and fear,
As the whispering echo grows.

In the heart, a truth resides,
Waiting for the moment right.
When the echo's call abides,
Be the beacon, be the light.

The Inner Sanctuary

Amid the noise and endless race,
Seek a quiet, sacred place.
Where your soul can reach its height,
In the warmth of inner light.

Find the silence, hear the call,
Of your heart and nothing more.
In that space, beyond the wall,
Peace is waiting at your door.

In the sanctuary deep,
Find a world of pure and true.
With each breath, your soul to keep,
In the quietude of you.

Sacred Reunion

Across the fields of time,
Two souls once lost in dreams,
Find each other in the whispers,
Of forgotten moonlit beams.

Hands that once were parted,
Join beneath the starry night,
In the dance of sacred union,
Two hearts merge in purest light.

Echoes of past lifetimes,
Resonate in tender sighs,
As they weave through the cosmos,
With love that never dies.

Symphony Within

In the quiet of the morning,
A symphony begins,
Within the heart's vast chambers,
Where silence softly spins.

Each beat a gentle cadence,
A rhythm deep and rare,
Composing melodies of thought,
Beyond the world's glare.

Harmony and dissonance,
Blend in perfect form,
Creating inner landscapes,
Eternal, safe, and warm.

Majestic Stillness

Beneath the gilded sunrise,
Mountains stand in grace,
Silent sentinels of time,
Guardians of this sacred place.

In the valley hushed and vast,
Nature's whispers softly weave,
Stories of the ancient past,
In every leaf and eve.

Majestic stillness reigns,
In the realm of earth and sky,
A timeless, tranquil domain,
Where all sorrows gently fly.

Eternal Return

Through the cycles of existence,
Life's grand wheel does spin,
In endless ebb and flow,
An eternal return begins.

From birth to death and back again,
We tread the cosmic path,
In the dance of endless change,
Beyond the earthly grasp.

Embrace each fleeting moment,
With grace and wisdom earned,
For in the heart of every soul,
Lies the truth of our return.

Unearthing Inner Riches

Beneath the stone, a treasure lies
In quiet dark, a spark concealed
Unseen by those who pass it by
A heart of gold, in shadows veiled

Through layers deep, the miner goes
With careful hands and mindful grace
A wealth of self, the search bestows
In caverns vast, an inner place

What glimmers soft in hidden earth
That waits to shine, once brought to light?
A trove of worth, of endless birth
Within the soul, a boundless sight

To dig within, to find the gold
In silent quest, we journey through
Unearthed, the riches manifold
The wealth within begins anew

Inner Vistas

In twilight's hush, where murmurs cease,
A landscape forms in gentle peace,
Quiet paths of thought unspool,
In silence, there's a nameless rule.

Dreams arise in shadowed grace,
A softer realm, an inner space,
Starlit whispers, tender glow,
Through inner vistas, spirits flow.

Where hearts compose a secret song,
An evening dance, serene and long,
Each step, a story, yet unread,
In mystic light, where souls are fed.

Amid this world of soft confines,
A truth unlocks, a heart enshrines,
In quiet night, the mind expands,
Through inner vistas, hold my hands.

Harmony Rekindled

In the tender breath of dawn,
Where echoes of the night are drawn,
Two hearts convene, as dreams unfurl,
In whispered realms, a secret world.

Time's gentle tide, it ebbs and flows,
In quiet streams, where silence grows,
Through gentle touch, and heartbeats' chime,
Harmony rekindled, beyond time.

In eyes that speak of boundless grace,
A journey found in each embrace,
The world fades out, a soft set vice,
Love awakens, pure and nice.

With every step in union traced,
A silent world by love replaced,
Through tempest's cry and tender breath,
Harmony rekindled, love's depth.

The Inner Tapestry

Threads of thought in quiet weave,
In silent realms where dreams deceive,
A tapestry of inner sight,
Woven in the hush of night.

Colors mix in tender blend,
Each strand a tale, a twist, a bend,
Through hidden depths, a story flows,
In inner minds where silence grows.

The fabric sways in twilight's light,
A vibrant dance, a peaceful flight,
In every fold, a secret lies,
In shadows deep, beneath the skies.

Through hands that touch the silken thread,
Our dreams are formed, our fears are wed,
In woven spells of thought's decree,
Behold the inner tapestry.

Rediscovering Inner Whispers

Beneath the din of life's refrain,
In quietude, where thoughts remain,
Gentle whispers, truth uncurled,
Rediscovering inner worlds.

Through halls of mind where echoes dwell,
In hidden nooks, where dreams swell,
A voice of past, a silent plea,
Rediscovering what could be.

In heart's abyss, so deep, profound,
In every beat, there lies a sound,
Familiar tones of yesteryears,
Rediscovering, calm and clear.

As shadows lift, the light reveals,
A truth within, the spirit heals,
Through whispered winds, the soul will soar,
Rediscovering whispers' lore.

Embracing the Inner Light

In shadows, the soul takes flight,
Whispering secrets softly bright.
Cloaked in darkness, fears ignite,
A spark becomes the guiding night.

Beneath the stars, dreams take hold,
Whispers of truths yet untold.
Through the void, brave and bold,
Illuminating hearts of gold.

In twilight's realm, visions blur,
But courage finds its fervent stir.
From within, all doubts deter,
Empowered, pure intentions purr.

Light cascades, a beam divine,
Inner strength begins to shine.
Every shadow's whispered sign,
Guided by a force benign.

Hope restored in every heart,
The light within a work of art.
In unity, we all take part,
Each soul a glowing, luminous chart.

Homecoming of the Soul

Journeyed far through time's embrace,
In search of a familiar place.
Every trial and every chase,
Leads back to an eternal grace.

Echoes trace our wander's call,
In the silence, hearts enthrall.
Faith to rise and never fall,
Returning to that sacred hall.

Paths converging, fates align,
Stars above in perfect sign.
In this moment, soul redefines,
Peace reclaimed in love's design.

Tattered wings now mended true,
With the dawn, a brand new view.
All the trials we've been through,
Lead us home, our spirit's cue.

Sanctuary of warmth and care,
Heartfelt whispers fill the air.
In this circle, we repair,
Home at last, our truths declare.

Rediscovering Unity

In the depths of nights serene,
Whispers of dreams quietly glean.
Hopes of unity softly convene,
In hearts where love's light has been.

Once divided, now we mend,
Threads of trust begin to blend.
In each other, we transcend,
On this path, we now depend.

Bridges built from strength anew,
Together we rise, a brighter hue.
In the morning's golden dew,
Shared dreams unfold, a shared view.

Gather close, the world aglow,
Unified in every flow.
Hand in hand, our spirits grow,
Truth in unity we bestow.

Voice and chorus, song and sound,
In harmony, we're deeply bound.
Rediscovered, love profound,
In this unity we are found.

Wholeness Reclaimed

In the fragments left behind,
Pieces of our past entwined.
From the shadows, we redefine,
Seeking wholeness, hearts aligned.

Through the trials, we have grown,
Healing paths so brightly shown.
Every scar and every moan,
In our souls, the truth is sown.

Courage lights the darkest night,
In our hands, we hold the fight.
Wholeness like a beacon bright,
Guides us back to inner light.

Unified, we rise and stand,
In this journey, hand in hand.
Every whisper, grain of sand,
Forms a loving, healing land.

Wholeness claimed, our spirits free,
Bound by love and unity.
In this truth, we always see,
Reclaimed within our destiny.

Awakening to the Core

In depths of souls, a fire grows,
Beyond the veil, where spirit flows.
Through layers thick, we seek to find,
The core of being, intertwined.

With every dawn, a path revealed,
In quiet hours, truths are unsealed.
The chains of old, we break as one,
An endless journey has begun.

Transformation, subtle and bright,
In shadows cast, we see the light.
The heart, the mind, no longer torn,
Through inner realms, we are reborn.

The whispering winds, they guide the way,
In silence deep, where we must stay.
To find the core, the spirit's shore,
Awakening now, forevermore.

Whispered Awakening

In twilight hours, whispers start,
A gentle nudge within the heart.
Soft echoes speak, in shadows' grace,
Awakening dreams, a tender place.

The moonlight bathes the world in glow,
In stillness, we begin to know.
A voice so faint, yet crystal clear,
The path ahead dissolves the fear.

With every breath, the whispers weave,
A song of hope we can believe.
In moments hushed, we find our way,
To dawns of new and brighter days.

Through whispered winds, our spirits rise,
With open hearts and opened eyes.
The call of soul, we hear and heed,
Awakening now, our truest need.

Sacred Realignment

In sacred spaces, realign,
Where spirit's peace and heart combine.
The veil is thin, the portal near,
In quietude, we see it clear.

The stars above, they gently guide,
Through cosmic waves, with every tide.
In unity, we're bound to seek,
The strength found in the kind and meek.

A dance of light, a sacred flow,
The ancient rhythms we follow.
In realms unseen, we find our place,
Realign with love's embrace.

The journey vast, yet inward drawn,
To realms where ego's veil is gone.
Through sacred paths, we reunite,
With all that's true, in love's pure light.

Harmonious Return

In harmony, the world returns,
As inner fire gently burns.
The symphony of life's refrain,
Resounds within, a sweet sustain.

The river flows with gentle ease,
Through valleys green and ancient trees.
In rhythm pure, we find our song,
A place where we have always belonged.

The seasons turn, the cycle spins,
As life renews, as love begins.
Through trials faced, in joy and pain,
We come to know our souls again.

With every step, our spirits yearn,
For unity, a safe return.
In harmony, our truths we find,
In love's embrace, forever intertwined.

Inner Landscapes

Within my mind, vast vistas spread
Mountains of thought arise
Rivers of hope meander steady
Beneath the azure skies

Echoes of dreams in valleys deep
Whispers of past and future
Painted with hues of fleeting time
Moments in silent capture

Forests of wisdom, tall they stand
Guardians of age and lore
Their roots sink deep in ancient soil
Stories forevermore

Plains of peace, an endless stretch
Horizon blends in light
Journey within, in quiet steps
'Neath starlit canopy night

Through deserts of despair, I trek
Oases found within
A mirrored world of soul's design
The frontier, where I begin

Touch of Serenity

A gentle touch, the morning breeze
It whispers through the trees
Carrying the scent of dawn so pure
A promise on its knees

The stillness of a quiet lake
Reflects the sky's embrace
In its calm, a heart finds rest
A mirror to its grace

Sunlight dances on the waves
A ballet of golden light
In each glimmer, serenity
A world reborn in sight

Mountains stand in silent guard
Their peaks a vow of peace
In their shadow, comfort found
Where bustling thoughts release

As twilight weaves its tender hue
The day's soft slow descent
In night's cloak, the touch of calm
A world at last content

Luminous Solitude

In solitude, a light is found
A beacon in the night
Guiding hearts through shadowed paths
To depths of endless sight

The stars alone in heavens wide
Each twinkle, a silent cry
Yet in their gleam, a dance unfolds
A beauty reaching high

The moon upon its solitary throne
Illuminates the sea
In every wave, a glistening dream
Of what it means to be

Through silent woods in midnight's veil
A glowworm's gentle spark
In quietness, it lights the way
For wanderers in the dark

Embrace the calm, the quiet glow
That solitude bestows
In luminous self-discovery
The inner light which grows

Inner Light Unfolding

Within the heart, an ember sleeps
Awaiting breath to rise
Awakening the inner flame
A star born in the skies

Through trials faced in darkest hour
A light begins to form
In adversities, strength unveiled
A glow both soft and warm

In silence, whispers of the soul
Speak truths that long inspire
A beacon where the spirit soars
A flame to ignite fire

The dawn within crescendos bright
Dispelling nights so cold
In rays of inner wisdom's might
A story to be told

So journey on through veils of doubt
For in your depths, you'll see
The inner light unfolding pure
A path to set you free

Inner Resurgence

Beneath the silent sky,
I find my hidden strength,
In shadows where I lie,
There's power in my length.

Rising from the deep,
A roar begins to form,
No longer shall I sleep,
I'll weather every storm.

Resilient hearts don't break,
They change and they renew,
For every step I take,
A clearer path in view.

The dawn's first gentle rays,
Illuminate my course,
Through winding nights and days,
I find my inner source.

I've danced with pain and grace,
Emerging from the fall,
In every scarred embrace,
I stand, I vow, I call.

Reclaiming Inner Light

In corners dark and vast,
Where shadows often play,
My light seemed lost and past,
Yet there it yearns to stay.

With courage I ignite,
The flames that fade no more,
Reclaiming all my light,
Unlocked through hidden door.

With clarity I'll stride,
Through fields of doubt and fear,
No longer shall I hide,
For inner light is near.

The whispers of my soul,
In stillness I embrace,
Each fragment makes me whole,
A radiant, glowing lace.

In every moment small,
A universe in sight,
I answer to the call,
And shine with pure delight.

Awakening the Inner Flame

When night feels cold and long,
And silence chills the air,
I find my inner song,
A warmth beyond compare.

The sparks of dreams alight,
Within my heart anew,
In darkness there's a light,
That guides my spirit through.

Through trials faced and fought,
My fire ever burns,
In lessons life has taught,
Each ember deepens, turns.

With passion fierce and bright,
I fan the flames inside,
Awakening the light,
Where hope and love reside.

As dawn dispels the night,
With colors bold and free,
My flame grows strong and bright,
It lives, it breathes in me.

Roots of the Soul

Beneath the surface deep,
Where ancient whispers stay,
The roots of soul still keep,
Their truth in earth and clay.

In every branch that thrives,
A story does unfold,
In timeless ties it lives,
Their secrets they behold.

Through seasons warm and chill,
They anchor and sustain,
With steadfast, constant will,
And strength through sun and rain.

Within the soil's embrace,
My spirit finds its ground,
In roots of time and space,
A peace therein is found.

As leaves ascend to skies,
Above the worldly strife,
My soul's deep roots arise,
To nourish all of life.

Spirits Reunited

Across the veils of time and space,
Two souls converge in a timeless dance.
Whispers of love in the winds of grace,
Their bond defies mere circumstance.

Eternal flames in the cosmic sea,
Guided by stars of destiny.
Together they roam, wild and free,
In realms where dreams find sanctuary.

A moment to part, yet always near,
Their essence entangled, pure and clear.
In the tapestry of life, no fear,
For love transcends each finite year.

Circles of life, an endless thread,
In every birth, the vows are said.
From cradle to grave, and where angels tread,
Their spirits reunite, never dead.

Within the Silent Depths

In the silence of the deepest night,
Where shadows dance with pale moonlight.
Secrets whisper, out of sight,
In silence, hearts take flight.

A whispered thought in a quiet mind,
In stillness, true connections find.
Lost memories of a kinder kind,
Within the silent depths, we're aligned.

Reflections in the mirror's glaze,
Quiet truths in the nightly haze.
Eyes that speak in a silent phase,
In the quiet, love's fires blaze.

In the calm of a wordless song,
We find the place where we belong.
With silent strength, forever strong,
In depths where right meets wrong.

Pathway to the Heart

Through winding lanes and pathways faint,
Lies the road adorned in love's own paint.
Every step, a refrain so quaint,
Leading to where hearts acquaint.

Beneath the canopy of reaching trees,
Whispers travel on a tender breeze.
Hands entwined in soft reprise,
A path unerring to appease.

In meadows of green, where flowers sway,
Petals spring where hearts convey.
Journeying souls find their way,
To the heart where love will stay.

Guided by stars in the evening's sheen,
A celestial path of the unseen.
In the journey, serene and keen,
Hearts unite in spaces between.

Restoring the Inner Temple

In the quiet of one's sacred space,
Where inner peace finds its trace.
Shadows fall, but leave no trace,
Within, we find abundant grace.

Walls of mind, once torn and scarred,
Heal with time, though they were marred.
Softly whispers the soul unbarred,
Restoring what was once too hard.

In sanctuaries of thought and dreams,
Where crystalline clarity gently gleams.
Rebuild the self through sacred streams,
In the temple's heart, there love redeems.

Every breath, a healing note,
Within our being, light will float.
On the soul's pure soft tote,
Harmonies of peace we devote.

Echoes of Remembering

In the quiet, whispers find me,
Shadows of a time long past.
Softly, memories unwind me,
Echoes of the love that lasts.

Old photographs, tattered edges,
Tell the stories, speak the names.
In their silence, truth pledges,
To rekindle long-lost flames.

Walking through the halls of yesteryear,
Footsteps light, yet filled with weight.
Every turn, a cherished tear,
At memory's eternal gate.

From the echoes, peace is borrowing,
In the stillness, hearts align.
In remembering, we are growing,
In the past, the future signs.

Heart's True Compass

In the depths of silent feeling,
Guided by an unseen force,
Is the heart, its secrets sealing,
Navigating love's true course.

Through the storms and winds it follows,
With a will that won't concede.
In the quiet, strength it hallows,
Planting hope with every seed.

North and south, the journey takes us,
West and east, horizons call.
Love's compass directs and makes us,
Stand together through it all.

In the quest, no path is certain,
Yet with heart, we find our way.
Every doubt becomes a curtain,
Drawn to show a brighter day.

Journey to the Center

Through the forests thick and wild,
Past the rivers, ever flowing,
Steps of both the meek and mild,
Seek the place of inner knowing.

Mountains tall and valleys low,
Guide the soul on paths untrodden.
Ancient wisdom starts to show,
Remnants of the truths forgotten.

In the stillness of the night,
Stars above illuminate.
In their glow, we find the light,
Timeless truths, our hearts relate.

To the center, paths converge,
Soul and spirit intertwine.
On this journey, we emerge,
Unified in the divine.

Sanctuary of the Self

In the quiet, find the haven,
Where the mind and spirit blend.
Waves of calm, sweetly engraven,
In the heart, where troubles end.

Walls of peace and floors of silence,
Building walls that never break.
In this space, no need for violence,
Only love for its own sake.

In the sanctuary, breathe deeply,
Feel the world dissolve away.
In its solace, rest completely,
Be the night and greet the day.

Inner peace, the mind's creation,
Home within, forever new.
In this place of meditation,
Find the self, both wise and true.

Unfolding Inner Dimensions

In the depths where silence grows,
Thoughts like whispers of the night,
Petals of the mind unclose,
Revealing truths in soft daylight.

Journey into realms unseen,
Where the heart and spirit blend,
Each glance within a fleeting scene,
A story with no end.

Threads of dreams and waking hours,
Woven in a seamless braid,
Unfolding inner hidden powers,
In shadows and the glade.

Layers peel beneath the skies,
As echoes of the soul arise,
Past the veils and through the eyes,
Seeing through our own disguise.

Inner worlds in silence bloom,
Depths of more profound hues,
Unfolding gently in the gloom,
A self that is both old and new.

Embracing Wholeness

In the cradle of the dawn,
We weave the threads of morning light,
Where each fragment is drawn,
Into a tapestry of bright.

Embracing each broken part,
With the gentlest of grace,
Healing every wounded heart,
In a compassionate embrace.

Where divides once held sway,
And shadows cast their long spell,
Unity dawns in a new day,
As separateness bids farewell.

Completeness found in the sum,
Of moments lived and lessons learned,
As whispers of wholeness come,
In every corner turned.

With each breath the circle closes,
In a dance both old and real,
Embracing wholeness as it proposes,
A beauty found in the healed and the healed.

Where Shadows Dissolve

Where shadows cast their spectral dance,
In realms where darkness holds its sway,
Light breaks through with calm romance,
    Turning night into dawn of day.

In the twilight's tender glow,
Wounds and fears begin to fade,
Miracles in the gentle flow,
Of love's unending serenade.

In the dim and silent corners,
Where echoes of the past reside,
Hope and peace become adorners,
Casting shadows far and wide.

Through the night's despair and sorrow,
A whisper comes soft and clear,
Promises of a new tomorrow,
In a world where love draws near.

Shadows dissolve in morning's ray,
Fragmented dreams weave and bind,
Bringing life into the fray,
Creating light within the mind.

In the dance of light and dark,
Balance finds its sacred role,
Where each shadow leaves its mark,
On the canvas of the soul.

The Quiet Reclamation

In the quiet's subtle grasp,
Where the world begins to still,
Answers found in the silent clasp,
Of whispers turned tranquil.

Lost amidst the fervent chase,
To reclaim the inner peace,
Gentle echoes find their grace,
In moments where the noises cease.

Nature's hymns in the morning dew,
Sing the song of reconnection,
Guiding hearts to something new,
A quiet reclamation.

The soul's journey to align,
With the harmony of the real,
In the stillness so divine,
True purpose we feel.

Reclaiming moments lost in haste,
In the stillness, life unfurls,
A quiet path that's interlaced,
With the beauty of our worlds.

Spirit Renewed

In twilight's calm, the mind reclaims
The tender balm of whispered flames.
Through valleys deep and mountains high,
A spirit soars beyond the sky.

The stars align in quiet grace,
Illuming paths we dare to face.
With hope reborn and courage true,
Old wounds they heal, and dreams renew.

In shadows past, where sorrows lay,
The dawn arrives, a brand-new day.
Within the heart, a fire ignites,
Dispelling fears, embracing light.

Through trials met and lessons learned,
The weary soul has now returned.
An endless well of strength is found,
In love's embrace, forever bound.

Veil of Serenity

Beneath the moon's soft, silver glow,
A tranquil river's gentle flow.
The stillness speaks in whispered tones,
As silence cradles ancient stones.

In meadows bathed in starlit beams,
We wander through our lucid dreams.
Ephemeral, the night unfolds,
With secrets quiet shadows hold.

The air is thick with nature's hymn,
A soothing breath on every limb.
Through tangled woods and fields untamed,
The heart finds peace, the soul reclaimed.

A symphony of quiet bliss,
Awaits within the night's sweet kiss.
Beyond the world's tumultuous sea,
Lies hidden deep, serenity.

Intrinsic Awakening

The dawn breaks forth with tender light,
Awakening the soul in flight.
From depths of self, the truth emerges,
A silent call, the spirit surges.

In mirrored lakes, reflections gleam,
Of dreams once lost, a hopeful beam.
The ancient oak, its roots profound,
Speaks tales of strength the earth has found.

Through inner realms, where shadows dance,
We find within a second chance.
To know oneself, a path so clear,
Through love and loss, we persevere.

In solitude, the heart expands,
Embracing all with open hands.
This journey inward, deeply sown,
Reveals a world we'd never known.

Rebirth of Clarity

In winter's chill, a seed is sown,
The promise of a life unknown.
Through icy storms and winds that wail,
Emerges bright, a tender trail.

Beneath the frost, where shadows creep,
The earth prepares a silent leap.
As sunlight dances, soft and pure,
The world awakens, reassured.

With every thaw, the rivers run,
To greet the golden face of sun.
In nature's breath, we find our way,
To futures bright and skies of gray.

A cycle ends, another starts,
Reviving dreams, rekindling hearts.
In clarity, a vision blooms,
Dispelling doubt, dispelling gloom.

Home in the Heart

The bricks are memories,
The walls, a whispering song,
Each corner holds a tale,
Where we truly belong.

Soft laughter fills the air,
Footsteps echo the past,
In the warmth of embrace,
Love like this always lasts.

Windows frame moments dear,
Doors open to delight,
Every room is a hug,
In days peaceful and night.

Shelves lined with dreams aglow,
Chairs worn by shared throng,
In this house of the heart,
Our spirits weave a strong bond.

Rooftop stars smile down,
Guardians of our lore,
In the heart, home is found,
A place forevermore.

Embrace of Stillness

Whispers of the morning dew,
In silence, secrets lie,
Nature's breath, a gentle coo,
Under the endless sky.

Moments pause in tranquil grace,
Time's soft touch, a guide,
In stillness, the world's embrace,
Where peace and calm reside.

Leaves fall in a quiet dance,
Seasons' silent play,
In stillness, there's a trance,
The night blends with the day.

Gentle waves kiss the shore,
A lullaby so sweet,
In the stillness, hear the lore,
Of heartbeats soft and neat.

A restless mind finds rest,
In nature's hushed domain,
In stillness, we are blessed,
Free from the binding chain.

Inward Blossoming

Within the soul, a bud,
Petals of dreams unfurl,
Soft whispers through the blood,
A dawning inner pearl.

Roots of love go deep,
Nourished by hopes so bright,
In shadows quiet they creep,
Emerging into the light.

The garden heart does grow,
With blooms of varied hue,
Inward blossoms overflow,
With resilience that renews.

Stems of courage rise,
Amidst a stormy sea,
Inward strength that defies,
Boundless, wild, and free.

In the mind's eye, flowers,
Gardens rich and vast,
Inwardly bloom powers,
In fields that ever last.

Symphony of Silence

In the quiet, a symphony,
Notes of tranquil sound,
A melody set free,
In the stillness, we are found.

Winds whisper through the trees,
A soft and gentle tune,
Rustling leaves, a breeze,
Under the silver moon.

Stars sing in silent space,
Voices of ancient light,
In silence, we embrace,
The music of the night.

Water softly flows,
A river's gentle song,
In its quiet, it shows,
Where harmony belongs.

In the silence, a grace,
A symphony so pure,
In stillness, we face,
A concert to endure.

Embrace the Inner Light

In shadows deep and night so still,
A spark within begins to spill,
Illuminate the path we trod,
Guided by the inner god.

Through storm and tempest, fears take flight,
We chase the dawn, the morning light,
No longer bound by doubt and dread,
A fire inside, by dreams we're led.

The world's harsh glare may blind our eyes,
Yet truth and hope from inside rise,
In every heart, a beacon bright,
Brave and bold, our spirits' light.

Beyond the dark, the light takes form,
In every soul, a quiet storm,
So hold the torch, and do not fear,
Embrace the light, the path is clear.

The journey long, a heavy load,
Yet deep within, a secret code,
Unlock the strength, release the fight,
Belief within makes darkness bright.

Finding Solace Within

Amidst the noise, the clamorous din,
A quiet place where peace begins,
Where thoughts align, and hearts can mend,
Solace found, the spirit's friend.

In whispered wind and gentle rain,
We find the balm for all our pain,
Inside the self, where silence grows,
The sanctuary, no one knows.

Through mindful breath and moments still,
We climb the steep, the daunting hill,
And at the peak, serene and clear,
The solace that we cherish dear.

From chaos' edge, we dive within,
To find the calm, the softest sin,
The ebb and flow of inner tides,
A tranquil state, by heart it guides.

Within the soul's deep, vast expanse,
A realm of dreams and beauty's chance,
So seek within, the quiet trails,
In solitude, true peace prevails.

Homeward Through the Soul

The winding road, so long and cold,
Yet home lies not in tales of old,
But deep within, where spirit thrives,
In soulful depth, our hope derives.

The place we seek, with every stride,
Is not afar, but deep inside,
In every heartbeat, every breath,
The soul's sweet song, defies all death.

Through landscapes vast and valleys wide,
We journey forth, with hearts our guide,
Yet in the end, we come to see,
The soul's embrace sets spirits free.

The quiet hearth, a gentle breeze,
A loving heart that aims to please,
In every smile, in every glance,
Our true home's found, by circumstance.

So walk the path, explore the land,
With open mind and outstretched hand,
For homeward bound, the way we see,
Is through the soul, eternally.

Reawakening the Spirit

Beneath the shadowed, dormant ground,
A pulse of life, a silent sound,
Awaiting spring to break the sleep,
A spirit stirs, in quiet keep.

The frost may linger, hearts may freeze,
Yet warmth returns on whispered breeze,
Awake the soul, to dreams anew,
In every heart, a dawn breaks through.

From depths of winter, cold and stark,
Emerges light, a single spark,
To reawaken spirits' fire,
And lift us from the darkened mire.

In every bud, a promise held,
A story of renewal spelled,
Through every trial, each darkened night,
The spirit rises, takes to flight.

Embrace the change, the seasons' turn,
In every heart, a fire to burn,
For reawakening is the key,
To live with soul, completely free.

Quiet Ascent

In silence, steps do softly tread,
Up the hills where dreams are fed,
Upon the path of whispers sound,
Peaceful journeys all around.

Moonlit skies guide tender feet,
Every star our gaze does meet,
Through the night, our spirits climb,
Ascending heights, defying time.

Breezes usher secret trails,
Through valleys and hidden vales,
Each ascent a gentle rise,
Whispers echo in the skies.

Morning breaks with amber hue,
Summit reached in clear view,
Quiet victory we have found,
In the hush, no louder sound.

Holding secrets, holding light,
Day and night in silent flight,
Quiet path, to skies we went,
Onward in our quiet ascent.

The Inner Renaissance

Within the heart, a spark does rise,
A phoenix from our own demise,
Renewal starts from deep within,
A renaissance where dreams begin.

Painted canvases of mind,
Brushstrokes of a different kind,
Reinvented, redefined,
Inward journeys now entwined.

Echoes of the past recede,
In the tide of every need,
Inner strength comes to the fore,
Breaking chains that held before.

Eyes now open wide and bright,
Seeing visions, pure delight,
Renaissance within the soul,
Making fragmented parts whole.

Inner worlds, landscapes of change,
Endless vistas, deeply strange,
Rising in this newfound dance,
Into the light of renaissance.

Blossoming Within

From the roots our essence grows,
In the soil where wisdom sows,
Deep within the hidden seams,
Blossoms form from cherished dreams.

Petals of the mind unfurl,
Inward gardens, thoughts do swirl,
Each new bloom a silent song,
Inner beauty, pure and strong.

Sunlight falls on leaves unseen,
Feeding hopes, fresh and green,
In the quiet, growth appears,
Blossoming through silent years.

Colors vibrant, shades unknown,
Inner gardens richly grown,
Blossoms light the inner face,
Graced by moments, full of grace.

Whispered winds of inner care,
Nurture blooms beyond compare,
In the stillness, life's within,
Blossoming shall now begin.

The Untraveled Path

Beneath the arch of ancient trees,
Lies the path few souls perceive,
Winding through the moss and shade,
Choices here are gently made.

Step by step, unheard, unseen,
Where no trodden prints have been,
Mysteries in shadows cast,
Serene and tranquil, unsurpassed.

Guided by the heart's own light,
Tiptoeing through the silent night,
The Unknown's map kept alive,
Here our spirits truly thrive.

Every turn a hidden gate,
Leading to another fate,
The untraveled path we tread,
By the soul's own quiet thread.

Venturing through realms anew,
In the heart, this path is true,
Footprints mark the journey long,
Through this path, our spirits strong.

Wholeness Redeemed

In the shattered space of time,
Peace and chaos intertwine.
Fragments once were lost and keen,
Now they form a perfect scene.

With shadows cast, the lights anew,
The broken pieces gently glue.
In the mending of what's been,
Find wholeness where the cracks had seen.

From depths of sorrow, joy will spring,
In harmony, the spirits sing.
Beyond the storm, the calm is beamed,
And life, at last, is redeemed.

The scars and marks they fade away,
As night turns into brighter day.
From darkest soil blooms a seed,
In every part, wholeness redeems.

So let the past not paint the dawn,
For every loss brings something born.
Embrace the whispers of the dream,
In every soul, wholeness redeemed.

Reconnecting the Threads

Woven tapestry of fate,
Threads of love and threads of hate.
In each stitch, a story bled,
Life's intricate, sweeping thread.

Through patterns lost and edges torn,
In tangled weave, new paths adorn.
Reconnecting what was said,
In silent whispers, threads are fed.

Beneath the fabric, shadows wane,
Connections brought, a gentle gain.
In each loop, the needle's dread,
Brings together broken thread.

Colors blend and stories merge,
In harmony, the patterns surge.
From chaos' art, creations wed,
Reconnecting every thread.

Time, the loom, and heart, the yarn,
Crafting tales by light and dark.
In stitches deep, connections spread,
Reconnecting, threads are led.

Inward Journey

The road within, a silent track,
Where echoes of the soul come back.
Through valleys deep and peaks unseen,
An inward journey, vast and clean.

In quiet moments, whispers low,
The self unveils what hearts don't show.
Through inner seas and skies between,
Discover realms where dreams convene.

The mind's vast ocean, dark and deep,
Where buried secrets lie and sleep.
In every wave, a thought is gleaned,
Inward journey, pure and gleaned.

Through shadows cast by worries high,
And fears that flutter in the sky.
In each step, the heart does glean,
Inward journey, mind serene.

Embrace the silence, let it be,
The guide to what's inside of thee.
In aloneness, spirit sings,
Inward journey, soul takes wing.

The Resonant Heart

Within the chest, a rhythmic beat,
A pulse where love and life do meet.
In every throb, a world apart,
Echoes from the resonant heart.

Through sorrow's storm and joy's retreat,
The heart finds ways to constant beat.
In the silent, darkened part,
Voice of the resonant heart.

Each emotion, a note distinct,
In harmony, their waves succinct.
In laughter loud or teardrop's dart,
Sings the song of resonant heart.

In connections deep, where souls entwine,
The heartbeats sync, a perfect line.
Love's symphony, its greatest art,
Plays within the resonant heart.

Though time may alter body's role,
The heart remains a constant soul.
Listen close, and feel the start,
Of life within the resonant heart.

Echoes of the Past Self

In distant shadows, whispers blend,
Old memories flicker, never bend.
Silent echoes of who we were,
Mingle with the present, a gentle stir.

Time's fragile tapestry unfurls,
Threads of history, in endless swirls.
Yesterday's whispers, today they sing,
Revealing the essence of everything.

Reflections in the mirror's glass,
Glimpses of a long-gone past.
A journey through the yesteryears,
Filled with laughter, marred by tears.

Phantom voices softly call,
Names and moments, we recall.
In the silence of the night,
The past and present reunite.

Through corridors of mind we tread,
Among memories, both bright and dead.
Echoes of the past self linger near,
In the present's glow, they reappear.

Ascension Within

In the silence of the soul's embrace,
Dreams of heights we dare to trace.
The path to stars, though steep and thin,
Is but a journey deep within.

Through forests dense and valleys low,
A guiding light begins to glow.
Each step forward, a soaring flight,
From shadows into purest light.

Climbing peaks of doubt and fear,
The summit's breath feels ever near.
In the heart, an ember burns,
A fire of strength, it brightly churns.

To ascend, look inside the heart,
Where journeys end and new ones start.
Within, the universe resides,
Through inner realms, the spirit glides.

In each ascent, a truth unfolds,
Of inner strength and dreams retold.
Upward we strive, beyond the din,
To find the heaven that's within.

Essence Unfolded

Within the core of every being,
Lies the truth we're often fleeing.
Unveil the mask, let essence flow,
Discover what we truly know.

Beneath the surface, deep and still,
Resides the force, the cosmic will.
A whisper pure, in silence told,
The mystery of the soul unfold.

Through layers dense, of doubt and fear,
A clearer vision starts to peer.
In shadows, light begins to weave,
The essence pure we then perceive.

Softly, petals turn and sway,
Inward journeys, night to day.
Each layer peeled, a story cries,
Of lives within our very eyes.

In every fold, a truth revealed,
The soul's pure light, forever healed.
Through inward paths, our selves we find,
The essence of the heart and mind.

The Quiet Revolt

In silent corners of the mind,
Revolts of heart, we often find.
A whisper loud, in stillness bred,
The quiet paths we dare to tread.

Not by shouts, nor raging fire,
But calm resolve and soft desire.
The quiet revolution starts,
In tender beats of restless hearts.

Through subtle moves and gentle sway,
We find a clearer, better way.
With every step, a purpose blooms,
In silent halls and quiet rooms.

A ripple in a placid stream,
Changes wrought in silent dream.
Whispered thoughts, with courage twine,
Mark the change, in hearts and minds.

In stillness, power truly lies,
A revolution 'neath the skies.
With quiet force, the strength we hold,
A gentle change, yet fierce and bold.

Core of Being

In the stillness of the soul,
Where whispers softly dwell,
A hidden truth unfolds,
Beneath the conscious swell.

Amidst the heartbeats' call,
Echoes of dreams ignite,
Ajourney to the core,
A beacon in the night.

The essence of our being,
In shadows often found,
Reveals the boundless light,
That silence can astound.

Within the self we seek,
A harmony profound,
Where universe and self,
In unity are bound.

Through time and space we flow,
On paths both near and far,
The core of our existence,
A radiant, guiding star.

Silent Revelations

In whispers soft as dawn,
The silent truths emerge,
With every breath a song,
A peaceful, gentle surge.

The secrets softly kept,
In twilight's quiet gaze,
Reveal the ancient steps,
Of life's mysterious ways.

In silent revelations,
Our deepest selves we find,
Each thought a constellation,
Within the vastest mind.

Through stillness we discern,
The echoes of our past,
In every quiet turn,
A wisdom meant to last.

The silence speaks of love,
Of truths we cannot see,
In every silent breath,
The soul finds liberty.

Inner Peace Found

Within the heart's embrace,
A tranquil river flows,
Through valleys and through space,
Where peaceful silence grows.

The storms of life may howl,
The winds of change may blow,
Yet deep within the soul,
A steady calm will show.

In moments softly still,
The inner self will bloom,
A garden on a hill,
Amidst the twilight's gloom.

With every breath we take,
A peace within is born,
A clarity that wakes,
In every rosy morn.

Through trials faced each day,
And challenges profound,
The heart will always say,
In peace, our truth is found.

Embrace of the Essence

In the quiet of the night,
Where shadows softly lie,
The essence takes its flight,
Beyond the earthly sky.

Through dreams we start to see,
The truth our hearts have told,
A dance of purest glee,
In visions bright and bold.

Embrace the inner light,
That dwells within our core,
It shines through darkest night,
Forever to explore.

The essence of our being,
A glow that never fades,
In every glance it's seeing,
The unity it wades.

With open arms we greet,
The truth that sets us free,
In essence we complete,
Our journey's destiny.

Self-Embrace Awakening

In the quiet dawn, I find my grace,
Amidst the stillness, my own face.
A journey within, to feel the warm,
Embrace of self, through life's storm.

Gentle whispers, my soul does speak,
In the shadows, no longer weak.
Beneath the layers, my true form lies,
A radiant sun in heartfelt skies.

Through tears and joy, I find my way,
Each moment, a new dance, a new play.
In the mirror, I see my friend,
A bond of love, no need to mend.

Awakening to the power inside,
No longer do I need to hide.
With open arms, I welcome me,
A journey of love, wild and free.

Within this heart, where peace does grow,
I nurture seeds of light to sow.
Self-embrace, a sacred art,
An endless rhythm from heart to heart.

The Inner Pilgrimage

Upon the path of silent tread,
A voyage within, where dreams are fed.
In the chambers of the heart, so deep,
Hallowed secrets, softly seep.

Each step a whisper, echoing true,
Guiding the soul towards what's due.
Through winding paths and shadow's dance,
A sacred journey, a soul's trance.

The mountains high, the valleys low,
In every trial, the spirit grows.
With courage fierce and eyes so wide,
Embracing all, with love allied.

Inward bound, the quest unfolds,
Treasures found in stories told.
The pilgrimage to one's own core,
Unlocks the light behind each door.

With every breath, a pilgrim's prayer,
To find oneself in depths laid bare.
Through inner realms, the spirit flies,
A sacred quest, where true self lies.

Echoes of Inner Harmony

In the silence, whispers rise,
A symphony beneath the skies.
Echoes of the heart now play,
Harmony in light's soft sway.

Silent strings of soul do weave,
Melodies that can't deceive.
In quiet moments, truth is found,
Echoes strong, a world unbound.

Through the chaos, peace does ring,
A timeless tune, the soul to bring.
In every note, the self does shine,
A harmony so pure, divine.

The echoes dance in endless flow,
A gentle song where hearts do grow.
In perfect sync, the spirit sings,
With every beat, new hope it brings.

In the stillness, hear the call,
A resonance that binds us all.
Echoes of the heart's pure song,
Guide us home where we belong.

Seeking Inner Horizons

Towards horizons yet unseen,
A journey where the soul does glean.
Through inner skies, the spirit soars,
Endless realms, through open doors.

Visions vast of inner space,
Where dreams and hopes find their place.
With every step, a new view forms,
In endless skies, where peace adorns.

Through trials faced and shadows cast,
Seek the light that everlast.
Inward bound, horizons call,
A journey rich, where fears do fall.

With open eyes, the soul explores,
New vistas found on spirit's shores.
The boundless depth of inner light,
Guides the seeker through the night.

Horizons near, horizons far,
A beacon bright, a guiding star.
In every heart, the journey lies,
Seeking truths where spirit flies.

Sanctuary of the Soul

In the quiet of the dawn,
Where whispers softly play,
A sanctuary of the soul,
Unfolds in gentle sway.

Gone are the days of strife,
Replaced by tranquil streams,
Where every heartbeat whispers hope,
And light beams dreamlike gleams.

Within this sacred space,
Peace blossoms, pure and full,
A refuge from the world outside,
A calm and gentle pull.

The soul finds its release,
In this serene embrace,
A sanctuary deeply nestled,
In boundless, timeless grace.

Beneath the tranquil skies,
Where solace takes its toll,
Lie the endless echoes found,
In the sanctuary of the soul.

Rediscovery of Self

In the mirror's quiet gaze,
A reflection starts to form,
Beyond the mask of days gone by,
A self begins to warm.

Each scar that's etched in silence,
Each dream that took its flight,
Unfolds in tender whispers,
In the stillness of the night.

Through trials and the darkness,
Emerges strength anew,
A rediscovery of the soul,
A spirit breaking through.

A journey to the inner core,
Where truth and essence lie,
Reclaiming pieces lost to time,
Beneath an open sky.

In the dance of shadows past,
And future dreams unfurled,
The rediscovery of self,
Embraces this new world.

Internal Trek

Through the forests of the mind,
Where shadows softly tread,
An internal trek begins,
With paths that intertwine and spread.

Each thought a winding trail,
Each memory a stone,
Steps taken one by one,
In solitude, alone.

Amidst the crests and valleys,
In the calm or the fray,
An inner journey unfolds,
Drawing night from day.

Seeking purpose, seeking peace,
Amongst the hidden lands,
An odyssey within the self,
With no set borderlands.

Traversing heart and spirit,
In an ever-deepening quest,
This internal trek reveals,
What the soul knows best.

Unseen Horizons

Beyond the edge of sight,
Where dreams and dawns entwine,
Lie unseen horizons vast,
Where hopes and stars align.

Each day a chance to venture,
Into the unknown vast,
To seek the unseen wonders,
And leave behind the past.

The winds whisper of places,
Where shadows do not fall,
A realm of endless beauty,
That beckons and enthralls.

Horizons spread their wings,
Inviting hearts to soar,
With promises of what may be,
And mysteries to explore.

In the dance of golden light,
Towards horizons grand,
Lies the journey yet unseen,
Ready to be spanned.

Resonance Within

In the quiet of the night,
Where shadows softly blend,
Whispers of the past ignite,
Moments start to mend.

Heartbeats echo dreams anew,
Beneath the starry gleam,
A symphony of life in view,
Reveals its hidden theme.

Woven threads of lost and found,
In the tapestry of time,
Each note, a subtle, sacred sound,
A silent, gentle chime.

Calling forth the souls who yearn,
For solace in the wind,
To the inner halls we turn,
Where true peace begins.

Resonance within the heart,
A melody so fine,
In this cherished space, a part,
Of something so divine.

Solitude Awakened

In the stillness of the dawn,
Where silent moments wake,
Solitude, a tranquil pawn,
In quiet steps we take.

Beneath the pale and gentle skies,
The world begins to turn,
Boundless beauty in disguise,
In solitude, we learn.

The whispers of a hidden breeze,
Through leaves of emerald hue,
Bring a sense of soothing ease,
A tranquil, rare renew.

In solitude, our minds can clear,
Of clutter, noise, and din,
Awakened heart and soul draw near,
To find the peace within.

Solitude, a treasured friend,
In life's chaotic sea,
Guides us gently to the end,
And sets our spirit free.

Depths of Inner Seas

Beneath the waves of consciousness,
Lies a world unseen,
Where thoughts dwell in endlessness,
In realms of blue and green.

The mind's seas, so deep and wide,
Harbor secrets dark and light,
Tides of time, they slowly slide,
Through both day and night.

Beneath the calm or stormy crest,
Hidden currents flow,
Guiding dreams through silent quest,
To places we don't know.

In the depths, we find our core,
Of wisdom, fears, and dreams,
The ocean's mysteries to explore,
In vast, eternal streams.

For in these depths, we truly see,
The essence of our soul,
Navigating life's grand sea,
To find our destined goal.

Peaceful Reflections

In the mirror of the lake,
Where skies and dreams unite,
Peaceful moments softly wake,
In dawn's gentle light.

Reflections of a tranquil mind,
Ripple through the still,
Echoes of the self we find,
In nature's quiet thrill.

Beneath the surface, clear and pure,
Truth and beauty hide,
In reflections, we assure,
Our spirit's gentle guide.

Hushed whispers in the twilight glow,
As day succumbs to night,
Peaceful moments ebb and flow,
In soft, harmonious light.

In the stillness, we reveal,
The essence of our being,
Reflections, pure and real,
In peace, our true seeing.

Illumination's Pathway

Through shadows deep the light does weave,
In tangled woods where secrets cleave,
A lantern held by unseen hand,
Guides wanderers across the land.

Whispers call from twilight's hem,
A beacon bright, a sacred gem,
Each footfall marks the journey clear,
Towards the dawn, where hope draws near.

Stars like torches light the skies,
Reflecting in the seeker's eyes,
With every step, the darkness fades,
Revealing truth in gentle shades.

The path is long, but strength renews,
With each new dawn, with morning's hues,
For in the quest, the heart finds peace,
And from confusion, sweet release.

So on we tread with spirits high,
Beneath the ever-watchful sky,
Illumination's guiding fire,
Fulfills the soul's most deep desire.

Veil of Understanding

A veil descends, so fine, so fair,
Spun from threads of dream and air,
It shrouds the mind in silken mist,
A mystery, both clenched and kissed.

Behind its folds, the world is new,
Colors blend in twilight's hue,
Shapes and forms both near and far,
Merge like whispers from a star.

Through this veil, we're taught to peer,
With hearts unclouded, vision clear,
To see the truths that lie beyond,
The hidden pools of wisdom's pond.

Each gaze unveiled, a lesson learned,
Each glance a story long yearned,
In understanding, we are free,
To grasp the silent symphony.

So lift the veil and start the flight,
Into the realms of soft twilight,
For there we'll find the common thread,
That binds the living to the dead.

Reviving the Essence

In the heart of winter's chill,
Lies a seed that slumbers still,
Waiting for the warming rays,
Of the sun's return, and brighter days.

In silence deep, it gathers might,
Dreams of blossom, dreams of light,
Roots extend to seek the dew,
Reviving essence pure and true.

From the earth, a tender shoot,
Springs to life in search of root,
Unfolding leaves like prayerful hands,
Greeting life with new demands.

Each day it grows, each night it rests,
Nature's rhythm in its chest,
Drawing forth from ancient ground,
The life that pulses all around.

So we too, from sorrow's night,
Can rise again to seek the light,
Reviving essence, heart, and soul,
To find ourselves, once more, made whole.

Celestial Harmony

Beneath the vast and starry dome,
The universe calls us home,
Each planet spins in silent grace,
Through the wonders of cosmic space.

Stars compose their timeless song,
An eternal melody, pure and strong,
Planets dance in rhythmic flight,
Bound by love's celestial light.

The moon's soft glow, the sun's bright flame,
Reveal the heavens' sacred frame,
In night's embrace, we find our place,
Among the stars, in endless space.

Galaxies swirl in grand ballet,
Time and space in vast array,
Each twinkling light, a distant voice,
In the symphony, we all rejoice.

Through the cosmic harmony,
We glimpse the truth of what must be,
A universe both wild and grand,
Held in the palm of love's own hand.

Heartbeats Rediscovered

In whispered dawns and twilight's grace,
We find the pulse of time's embrace,
With every breath, a tale unfolds,
In silent beats, life retold.

Through shadows cast and sunlight's gleam,
We navigate through every dream,
In heartbeats soft, and moments rare,
Rediscovery's gentle care.

Beneath the stars and morning dew,
Unveil the paths both old and new,
Where love once lost, again we find,
In rhythms of the heart, entwined.

Hope's echo dances on the breeze,
A symphony that never flees,
In every touch, a world awake,
With each heartbeat, the past we break.

Eternal whispers fill the night,
Guiding steps with subtle light,
In heartbeats found, our stories penned,
New chapters start, no end.

Horizons Inside

Beyond the skies, within our soul,
Lies a horizon, vast and whole,
Infinite dreams and whispered lore,
A universe within our core.

In every thought, a sunrise blooms,
Dispelling doubt and shadowed gloom,
With inward gaze, the journey starts,
To landscapes deep within our hearts.

Mountains high and valleys low,
In inner worlds, their secrets show,
Through winding paths of pure desire,
We'll find the spark, the inner fire.

Eclipsing fears with courage bright,
We trek through shadows into light,
The horizon's edge, a line we cross,
Exploring self, not feeling loss.

In realms within, we'll bravely roam,
Discovering places we call home,
Each step reveals the boundless tide,
Of endless horizons found inside.

Epiphany of Presence

In moments still, the truth is clear,
Epiphany of now draws near,
Each breath a gift, each heartbeat calls,
Presence wraps in silent thralls.

The fleeting past, the anxious 'morrow,
Dissolve into the now we borrow,
In present's touch, the soul finds rest,
A gentle calm within the chest.

Amid the noise, in quiet find,
The essence of a tranquil mind,
With every sigh, with every glance,
Dances the now, our purest chance.

Awake to life in vibrant hues,
The present's song, our hearts infuse,
No need to chase what once has been,
Epiphany lies deep within.

Eternity in moments small,
The presence hears and answers all,
Listen close to whispers keen,
Epiphany in presence seen.

Essence Unveiled

Beneath the surface, deep and true,
Essence shows in purest hue,
In silence, stillness, we perceive,
The hidden truths we all believe.

Through layers thick of doubt and fear,
The essence calls, so crystal clear,
In moments hushed, the soul reveals,
A truth that time and space unseal.

With gentle hands, pull back the veil,
Essence shines, will never fail,
In every heart, a light bestowed,
A guiding star on life's long road.

Unveil the spirit's core inside,
Where love and hope and dreams reside,
In every step and every breath,
Essence lives beyond all death.

So listen to the inner call,
Essence lies within us all,
In unveiled truth, our spirits soar,
In essences forever more.

www.ingramcontent.com/pod-product-compliance
Lightning Source LLC
LaVergne TN
LVHW051955060526
838201LV00059B/3659